To Wizzle,

I hope you enjoy
there poems

the last
word
before the call

for the ones who tell us no.

and for the ones who keep on.

the last
word
before the call

contents

Word to the reader

Writing is both audacious and absurd. Audacious in that you pursue a passion with which you believe you can change the world. Absurd because even though you know you probably can't - for greater writers have tried yet the world remains as it is - you still continue anyway.

Writers do not write for sport. It is not a flexing of the muscles. Not a battle of the ego or an exercise in self-indulgence. Writers do not write because they want to write better than, or to claim that they are the best writer since. They are not aiming to snatch a crown or to claim a throne. They write because there is a relentless fire; a kind of perpetual burning or a harrowing heat ravishing them from the inside out. An eternal internal combustion. An explosion. One that is only cooled with the telling of a story. The story never told.

Who would exchange for this life of enduring agony? Of self-deprecation? A torrential torture like bullet rain on the dome. Who? It is those with a quiet courage. A silent bravery. This person resides in all of us.

It is the dreamers and the believers, but not of themselves, more so, of each other. Of that which has yet to be but is slowly on its way. We hear it in quiet breathing. It is those whose story is untold.

Writing is resistance. Literature is liberation. We write to remember; we write to never forget.

be still for i am writing you
into all that i know

eternal reflection

i am

the manifestation of the consciousness

of my mother.

the perpetuation of the will of my father.

the genetic heretic tongue twisted shifted misfit.
cataclysmic intrinsic instinctive mystic. i've got scribes
who reside on the inside of my eyes so when i look up i
see parables written across the skies.

i walk the streets at night

and when i whisper to the darkness

my words bring out the light.

so i write. i write to free minds

that are trapped like deer caught in headlights. when i step

to the mic

i'll make wings grow out of your ears

so you will hear how i'm fly.

i spent years in the basement

patiently waiting

deconstructing philosophies

from the teachers and the laymen.

i decoded the statements;

religious theology from African spirituality

and retraced my history from the present to the ancient.

read manuscripts on papyrus

rose from the ground like Lazarus.

returned to the metropolis

witnessed angels at the station.

still trying to make an entrance.

it's hard to keep the faith

when bad intentions

are masked with good features.

it's hard to find heaven

when the pimps look like the preachers.

it's hard to gain knowledge

when students know more than teachers.

and everybody's in it for self.

stealing the wealth. killing the health.

can't find heaven cos we're living in hell.

stuck in a cell. with sinister ministers.

we're commuters to computers with no story to tell.

when did we forget to live life?

what do you see when you look in the mirror

into your own eyes?

i've got emotions running high

on a level you couldn't gauge

felt my dreams smash with rage

like drunken fists through windows panes.

it nearly shattered my whole life.

i remember sitting late at night

inches between a vein and a knife

but i had to redefine and find

the meaning of my life

and i came to find there's a thin line

between getting it close and getting it right.

a thin line between fight and flight.

a thin line between losing your vision

and gaining insight.

so with precision i made an incision

to the depths of my soul

and there i found a pad and a pen

and a voice spoke low it said

it is your destiny to write. don't be afraid my friend.

so i picked up the pen and began to write

and released the emotions that i had inside

it hit me so hard i started to cry.

i started to cry scriptures

and began to bleed prose.

i sniffed lines with my nose

like crack fiends i was addicted.

i wrote my dreams on concrete streets

i was afflicted. i heard the whisper

of the winds verses blowing in the breeze

bringing forgiveness like a priest

to the sinners on their knees.

i read nature's stories in the leaves of a tree.

Her only wish is that we learn how to live

peacefully. on one of my idle days

i saw my name written on a bible's page

and i was a disciple that sat around the table

on the last day and i had looked Him in the eyes

but when the paintings where drawn

my face was drawn in disguise.

still i rise.

i'm pulling stars out of the skies

they burn the lines

in my palm. i see the light in your eyes

and it brings me to calm.

i want to be free.

for what kind of life is this

if we're not free to dream?

if we're not free to believe

in the things that are meant to be?

we're all looking for peace.

remember first to look inside.

peace begins with peace of mind.

and if we piece together the pieces

in this puzzle of life

we'll see that peace is the missing piece

that we all need to find.

in our reflection.

prodigal son

return like the prodigal son.

word to the one

your beauty deserves homage

like the glow of the sun.

from the stars to the moon

the highest point in the noon

we'll pave a way never delay

for our journey is true.

this is spiritual.

in every sense a higher virtue

no need for rituals

for love alone dictates what we do.

close my eyelids

reminisce on nights searching for Isis.

Osiris.

a god i was

but now just blinded.

reminded of better days

living through the darkest haze

looking for hope.

fighting fears.

waiting for the light of brighter days

that exists within us.

and goes on without doubt.

what do you do

when you're trapped in but feel left out?

when you're giving minimum

but you feel maxed out?

sometimes you need to question

what life is about?

and when you're running

but you only run from yourself.

this world's view of heaven

is kind of like my hell.

i still see things that make

my heart swell.

we've all got a story to tell

so i stand to the side

shared my vision with the blind

sang a song with the deaf.

made sure i move right

so i stepped to the left.

now i walk with each step

on the road less travelled

mysteries unraveled

i was picking up boulders

like it was gravel.

on journey through space and time

looked up realised that His face was mine

He said *take your time. soon you will find*

and the day will come.

you can't know where you're going
unless you know where you're from.

i found hip hop

i found hip hop. lying in a comatose state
on a cassette tape labelled 1998
so i put it in the radio and pressed play.
and the first place i heard hip hop
was in my mother's voice.
the weight of her pain was too heavy
for her words to explain but i could see it written clearly
across her face.

i kept looking. and i found hip hop.
an ancient tradition now sold out by capitalism so the only
return we get on an investment is cash money, 50 cent and
2 chains.

i found hip hop. on a runaway slave with two chains. one
around his feet the other around his brain. so go figure
and excuse me that i still feel the pain

if someone calls me and says *that's my n...*
because on them ships they used to say
that's my n... think quicker. history is bigger
than cultural appropriation. i am African;
we are one people from many nations.

i found hip hop. in the struggle.
in the Haitian rubble and the Congo mist.
Olympic podium clenched fist. the war cry
of Toussaint L'Ouverture and Dessalines.
the poetry of Patrice Lumumba's
Independence Day speech. and the flow
of a Thomas Sankara freestyle on the roads
of Burkina Faso.
but now brothers on the corner getting lean.
leech on the blood that flows in the veins
of a crack fiend trying to forget the pain.

the day a pregnant teen makes her way

to the abortion clinic turning her womb

into a tomb. her cervix into a cemetery.

too soon. more warriors we lose. the truth

we choose to confuse from the lies.

i found hip hop. on the estates.

scriptures scratched inside dodgy lifts. broken gates.

graffiti etched on walls like hieroglyphs.

grandmother carrying the family's shopping

up the stairs on a rainy day.

started from the bottom means nothing

if your people are still there.

so what is even hip hop now anyway?

hip is the knowledge.

like the construction of the pyramids.

spiritual mathematics. the Ishango bone
of the Bantu Kongo.

hip is the knowledge.
like the school kid
who gets sent out of class
because they ask challenging questions.
hip is the education
that we never receive from the mainstream institutions.

hop is the movement.
like Gil Scott Heron; *the revolution will not be televised.*
hop is the movement.
like Marcus Garvey had 6 million followers worldwide.
hop is the movement.
hear the footsteps of sisters
who lead the revolution;

Yaa Asantewa. Kimpa Vita.

and Nanny of the Maroons.

if we're not careful

they'll do to hip hop

just like they did jazz and blues.

you'll recognise the sound but you won't

know its roots.

so to hip hop you've got to stay true.

hip hop is the knowledge and movement.

hip hop is you.

i'm talking about *hip hop*

so don't act *Like You Never*

heard *The Thieves Banquet*

Kill The Radio. The People know.

it's *Common Sense*

that *There Is A Light.* a *Black Star*
that shines *Below The Heavens.*
we've got the *Blueprint* to the constellations.
Brand Nubians on astral navigation
across the skies. *Black On Both Sides*
of the universe. *Jeanius* is the gift
and the curse of humanity.
in *My Country i'm out for presidents*
to represent me (say what?!).
i'm out for presidents to represent me.
i'm out for presidents to represent me.
i'm out for dead presidents to represent me...

i didn't find hip hop. hip hop found me.

politics 101

what kind of world are we living in?
where fat cats get paid dividends
on investments they made
lying cheating and stealing.
and at the bottom you've got kids
as drug dealers but at the top
pharmaceutical companies make millions
manipulating disease and illnesses.

i once heard someone say
if you're rich you get to live.
our state of mind is poor
like we've got nothing left to give.
it's like we're stuck in the wilderness
cannibalistic tendencies living like savages
in an environment so primitive a knowledge
so limited because we still can't figure out

how they built the pyramids
but we call *this* civilisation.
we have nations who order
the torture and slaughter
of innocent lives across the water.
perpetrating lies without purpose.
perpetuating lies in a media circus.
this is modern day colonisation.
a symbiotic invasion. an occupation
by nations causing chaos and disorder.
globalisation is their vision.
enforcing the laws of capitalism
across all foreign lands.
wage war. strategy four. reward those
who conform to their system. and silence
the voices of those who oppose or won't listen.
but the cataclysm's got our tongue

so we stay silent. just sit back and watch

but even the hands on a broken clock

are right twice a day so when they tell us

what time it is we accept what they say.

remember when they said it's time for change?

well what's changed?

it's just a change of face on the same game.

presenting the same claim.

inflicting the same pain.

collecting the same gain.

they wreak havoc for the black gold.

it doesn't matter

how many lives they have to take.

how many homes they have to break.

how many enemies they create.

it's all for the oil's sake.

because oil translates

into capital.

so they move in on capitals.

just so they can cap it all.

this is politics 101 with a capital P.

first lesson is:

don't trust what you read in the news

or what you see on TV.

refuge

imagine how it feels to be chased out of home.
to have your grip ripped. loosened from your
fingertips something you so dearly held on to.
like a lovers hand that slips when pulled away
you are always reaching.

my father would speak of home. reaching.
speaking of familiar faces. girl next door
who would eventually grow up to be my mother.
the fruit seller at the market. the lonely man
at the top of the road who nobody spoke to.
and our house at the bottom of the street
lit up by a single flickering lamp
where beyond was only darkness. there
they would sit and tell stories
of monsters that lurked and came only at night
to catch the children who sat and listened to

stories of monsters that lurked.

this is how they lived. each memory buried.

an artefact left to be discovered by archaeologists.

the last words on a dying

family member's lips. this was sacred.

not even monsters could taint it.

but there were monsters that came during

the day. monsters that tore families apart

with their giant hands. and fingers that slept

on triggers. the sound of gunshots ripping through

the sky became familiar like the tapping of rain fall

on a window sill.

monster that would kill

and hide behind speeches, suits and ties. monsters

that would chase families away

forcing them to leave everything behind.

i remember

when we first stepped off the plane.

everything was foreign. unfamiliar. uninviting.

even the air in my lungs left me short of breath.

we came here to find refuge. they called us refugees

so we hid ourselves in their language

until we sounded just like them.

changed the way we dressed to look just like them.

made this our home until we lived just like them

and began to speak of familiar faces. girl next door

who would grow up to be a

mother. the fruit seller at the market.

the lonely man at the top of the road

who nobody spoke to. and our house

at the bottom of the street

lit up by a single flickering lamp

to keep away the darkness. there

we would sit and watch police that lurked

and came only at night

to arrest the youths who sat and watched police

that lurked and came only at night. this

is how we lived.

i remember one day i heard them say to me

they come here to take our jobs

they need to go back to where they came from

not knowing that i was one of the ones who came.

i told them that a refugee is simply

someone who is trying to make a home.

so next time when you go home,

tuck your children in and kiss your families

goodnight, be glad that the monsters

                              never came for you.

in their suits and ties.

                              never came for you.

in the newspapers with the media lies.

                              never came for you.

that you are not despised.

and know that deep inside
the hearts of each and every one of us
we are all always reaching
for a place that we can call *home*.

this is not just

this is not just
another war.
not just another group of rebels fighting
without a cause. puppets on a string. stealing
riches from a nation's poor.
people suffering. *this is not just*
another fight. not another plight of a people
as the screams of teenagers echo
into the night.

we've turned pages in history.
gone from dark ages into the light
but *this is not just*
another struggle that we will one day
leave behind.

not just

another thought on the back

of our minds as long it doesn't interrupt

with our lives, we choose

only that which our conscience can bare. we lose

our humanity

every time we stare at a television.

every time we eat in McDonalds.

sat by the window seat of a Starbucks

with a cappuccino reading the latest pop book.

every time we download an app

on our iPhone. iPad.

i am alone.

this is not just

 what happens here to the little girl

broken to pieces hiding her tears.

never allow your fears

to be greater than your dreams.
i rarely cry but every time i write
i shed streams. *this is not just* poetry.
this is a prayer. this is eyes closed
bended knees hands together in the air.
this is for every struggle in humanity.
from the Middle East to East Congo
we are not alone.

this is not just for me.
this is for the homeless person
begging on the streets.
this is for the single mother.
the clinically depressed.
the war child: post-traumatic stress disorder.
the daughter of a rape victim.
this is for the ones who cry.

and for the ones who hold it all in.

the beautiful ones who are not yet born.

this is for the ones

who struggle their whole lives

and will only know scorn.

this is to humanity.

this is not just.

they say this is for freedom

yet they kill for peace.

they hate for love.

fill our lives with lies.

indoctrination so we now despise

everything

including the truth though

we barely recognise what it is.

we no longer dare to live.

instead we hide.

behind screens. online. out of sight.

we intellectually verbalise

premature ejaculation

how can this be pro-creation?

when we abortion everything

including our dreams.

somebody please tell me what it means

when it seems you're the last one

who really cares?

so many hollow eyes that stare

back at you

souls drifting into the sea

sinking in the depth.

i would dare to give my next breath

if it would be the seed

that would grow the tree of life

so we could live again.

but i cannot make that sacrifice.

i am not Horus. Krishna. Christ.

i cannot Atlas this world onto my shoulders

when finger tips on revolvers

are the decision makers.

when the lease of life is held upon a holster

and fate is decided

by the distance

between the hand to the hip. sometimes

the best i can do is cry.

so i cry

for the 99 times whips cracked on backs

and rubber bullets.

triggers and the 99 fingers that pull it.

for the 99 families that mourn with every

sunrise. and the 99 women just raped

in an eastern Congo village.

the blood and oil spillage.

for the 99 miles of coastline

destroyed by nuclear waste. and the 99 times we were

promised a change that never came.

i cry.

these tears are my cocoon

and every 99 days

i am reborn trying to find the balance

between the heavy and the light

but the weight weighs down on me

so i wait for a way to weigh these ways

so i can wei-wu-wei philosophically back

to where i need to be. into the ether.

for this world isn't mine.

i barely recognise what it's become.

what will i do when that day comes

when my first born son will look at me and say

da*d, what happened to humanity?*

with my nervous hands and trembling tongue

before my heart finds its feet

and jumps out of my chest

i'll put down my cape

and remove the superman complex

that seems to come with fatherhood.

then i can only hold my breath

and hope to find the words

that will deflect the pain that he will feel

when he realises that this world was stolen from him too.

after all what can I say?

Son…

where we wait for god

a thousand hands clamped together

like scaffolding, holding up a building

of prayers.

where inside lives dreams of children growing.

flowing like water. streams of hope

for pencils in hands before guns.

of fields of flowers. daffodils and dandelions

before land mines. bombs stepped on

limbs torn apart like trust in a family feud.

of market sellers. women with blues

written on their skin. the food

they sell is faith for the futures of their daughters that they

may understand

their fate is more than

just to marry their husbands or to be raped

by rebels or soldiers.

we wait for God.

with Jesus perched on the edge of lips

hanging at the end of every sentence

like lynched black bodies from a tree

or the smile of a new born child.

this bittersweet, damning salvation

this imprisoning liberation, this despair

hope

to be free.

we

wait beneath clouds; rain falls down

like bullets in the east.

little boys with empty stomachs

in mines digging for currency.

money does not grow on trees

it grows in the ground but it is

always someone else

who eats

always someone else

who feasts

always someone else

with peace.

we

speak of this war but the cries fall

on deaf ears so we wait for a god with ears

like ripe soil so we can plant these prayers

and watch them grow. but we are still waiting

a thousand hands clamped together

holding up a country.

home is where the humanity is.

where black bodies die (and the world doesn't seem to care)

in cells. face down on concrete
floor. hood up.
6 shots. 9 shots. choked.
i can't breathe
or *please*
don't shoot.

washed up on shores.
Libya. Somalia. Nigeria. Sudan.
empty stomachs. ropes around throats.
watch them hang.
800'000. 2 million. 6 million.
Congo. on fields.
in mines, for phones.
on boats. ships.
thrown overboard. drowned.

bottom of the ocean.

in front of eyes

that look the other way.

a different violence

it is one thing to be killed. left

for hours on cold concrete.

choked until your black is blue. beat

to a pulp. chalk outlined from

6 shots. 9 shots. even shots whilst you sleep.

rough rope on smooth of skin. hanging.

but to have to change your voice.

the way you speak. to talk like *this*.

to always have your hands shown.

to wear your hair any way but how it grows.

to leave your *self* at home. and wear that smile. that suit.

shirt and tie. because it makes you look less.

you. to shrink. to change the way you think.

to publicly apologise for that crime

you had no involvement in. to remind

them that you are not like *them*.

to have to fit in.

this is a different kind of violence.

tell them (they have names)

and when they turn the bodies over
to count the number of closed eyes.
and they tell you 800'000: you say
no. that was my uncle. he wore bright
coloured shirts and pointy shoes.

2 million: you say *no. that was my aunty.*
her laughter could sweep you up like
the wind to leaves on the ground.

6 million: you say *no. that was my mother.*
her arms. the only place i have ever
not known fear.

3 million: you say *no. that was my love.*
we used to dance. oh, how we used to dance.
or 147: you say *no. that was our hope. our future.*

the brains of the family.

and when they tell you
that you come from war: you say
no. i come from hands held in prayer
before we eat together.

when they tell you that you
come from conflict: you say
no. i come from sweat. on skin.
glistening. from shining sun.

when they tell you
that you come from genocide: you say *no.*
i come from the first smile of a new born child.
tiny hands.

when they tell you

that you come from rape: you say

no. and you tell them about every time

you have ever loved.

tell them that you are from mother

carrying you on her back.

until you could walk. until you could run.

until you could fly.

tell them that you are from father

holding you up to the night sky. full of stars.

and saying *look, child. this is what you are made of.*

from long summers. full moons.

flowing rivers. sand dunes.

 you tell them that you are an ocean

that no cup could ever hold.

do i scare you?

does my frame evoke memories

of 1990s tabloid newspapers?

does my skin impregnate your mind

with thoughts of what i might be like?

flashing images of Brixton circa 1981

before my time. Tottenham 2011. or tomorrow?

do i remind you of a history you never knew?

that my bloodline injected existential philosophy

into the comatose stages of *the dark ages*

erased from pages his story that was never told.

do i scream *Mandela* into your ear drum?

or shout *Congo* as you key into your cellular phone?

does my smile send tremors of dichotomy

to your epicentre

rupturing the placenta that almost gave birth

to your fear?

or is it just me?

not enough

it is not enough to pray

for even in the scriptures it says

help yourself and the heavens will help you.

and though it is believed God spoke the world

into existence in 6 days even He had to

get on His knees and use His hands

to create humanity. even slaves

who used to pray for freedom

used their feet to run away and make their dream

to be free a reality. now what about us?

we cannot just sit and let the scriptures gather dust

in our guts. muted

like the muffled screams of orphaned babies

kidnapped from parents murdered in war

we must spit it up. for the word alone is not enough.

it is not enough to sit and wait

for the day

that someone may come and save us.

there is no salvation but the one we find

within when we give meaning and purpose

to our lives. and we make the sacrifice for

ourselves. for each other.

is it not enough that 6 million have gone

and returned their bodies to earth?

what is this death without witness?

that the world could not even look once.

what have we learned?

and how can we speak of *never again* when

more and more bodies keep falling to the ground

the cries become too familiar;

just a hollow murmur.

a soft dullness of sound.

is it not enough that i once saw a picture

of a little boy with soft tender hands. tender.

pleading

with fingers like the stems of flowers.

his palms. red like rose petals.

red. from the blood of carrying his dead father.

lifeless. through the ground.

pleading

that life may find him once again

and i cried for him

because i would give him the world if i could.

but someone said to me that i should pray

for the boy to have strength but what strength

can i pray for him if i do not even know if he is still alive?

and i cried. i cried.

so what strength do i even have left?

is it not enough that women have had their bodies

mangled and mutilated by the destruction of men?

with eyes like wrecking balls

and fists that pump like pneumatic drills.

pumping and crushing to pieces women's bodies;

the temples churches and mosques

where we all prayed as children to our gods

and found heaven at their feet.

these walking constellations. women's bodies.

we turn them into coffins. morgues. mausoleums.

where we bury our dead.

this poem is not enough.

if all it does is make us sit uncomfortable

whilst reading. and we let these words pass through us like

ghosts. 6 million ghosts.

6 million forgotten souls and

                                        we forget.

as soon as we leave *here* and return

to the mundane of our lives.

                                      we forget.

switch on our televisions.

                                        we forget.

go shopping on the high street.

                                        we forget.

on our computers and mobile phones.

                                        we forget.

i hope these words rest

and sit uncomfortably like glass

on the back of your throats

so that every time you speak

you feel it cut you so deep

 you can only talk of the pain.

this pain. it won't go away.

it lives in us. in our blood. in our guts.

maybe

we need to cut ourselves open

but still it would not be enough.

l'humanité

l'humanité est perdue.

convaincu que les illusions nous voyons

sont vrai

mais c'est une fausse réalité.

une nature corrompue.

dirigée par la haine et la cupidité.

une lumière dans l'obscurité.

le conflit et la guerre ;

oppression dans la rue.

oppression militaire.

oppression scolaire.

dans les écoles l'intelligence est perdue.

on a construit des pyramides

c'était les étoiles qui nous guidaient.

une puissance solaire.

divine.

la sagesse de l'univers.

gardez vos traditions et la terre.

gardez les façons de vos ancêtres.

n'oubliez pas votre mission.

sachez votre raison d'être.

l'humanité est Africaine :

l'humanité humaine.

l'humanité elle est où?

on est attrapé par les chaines;

le capitalisme. le nouvel esclavagisme.

les chaines mentales sont plus fortes

que les chaines physiques.

dans la nuit j'entends les cries des enfants.

comprenez que ce à nous de leur donner

un nouveau monde.

qu'est-ce que ça va être encore?

des cauchemars ou des rêves ?

l'amour ou la haine ?

le début ou la fin?

il faut que l'humanité revienne.

i dream of peace

a peace that fills streets
with a rhythmic beat
from the skipping feet
of little children on their way to school.
and to that same beat we'll dance.

a peace that opens many doors
and where one day
words like war
will be a thing of the past.
children will look back and laugh
and say *people don't die that way*
anymore.

a peace where
physically mentally or spiritually
there is no rape.

where men do not break

women's hearts or shatter their minds

because that kind of peace

is the most precious that a man can find.

i dream of a peace where

buildings will not crumble as the earth rumbles.

and where any boy in the world

can one day grow up to be the next

rumble young man rumble.

stories will be told from far and high

about how during the most roughest times

you and i were unified.

and from our path we did not stumble.

we will one day know for whom the bell tolls

but that bell will bring a peace
that fills our hearts with a song
silenced for far too long.
it doesn't matter where you're from
dream of a peace where you can go anywhere
in the world and you will belong.

a peace where birds are let free
from their cage and we're no longer held
prisoner by rage. the innocent no longer placed
behind bars carrying physical wounds
or psychological scars
for the cry of justice will be heard
from both near and far
on that day when peace is all of ours.

peace.

my religion

we are the sum of all our life experiences.

every breath that we have taken is enough

to set off a hurricane that lifts cities by their skyline.

every beat of our hearts

has enough rhythm to move

all the dancing feet trying to find

their way home. every time we have ever loved.

i dreamt of us. sitting in quiet moment.

our thoughts. in silence. our words.

i listened. you breathed.

i watched. your eyes.

they magicked. light

from the moon until it found us.

your smile was poems

written by an illiterate blind muse

who could only see with his hands.

knowing those images would fade
if he stopped feeling.
he made the very best of you.

you are the very best of you.
even god had to pray to the best parts of Herself
to make you. i am glad that you are here.
for your being here right now is
by no accident. it is a testament
to every struggle you overcame.
every time you found a way.
every time you were trapped in the
darkest hour of the night
but still found the light of day.

my mother told me
that i would one day fall in love.

i told her that my fists are full

and my heart is too heavy

so love is a burden that i cannot bear to carry.

she said *let go of your fears and make room.*

little did i know she was talking about you.

the world sits on its axis

because even it tilted its head in awe

when it first saw you. when i first saw you

my eyes became disciples to your beauty

converting my mouth to speak only of your

truth. love.

this is my religion.

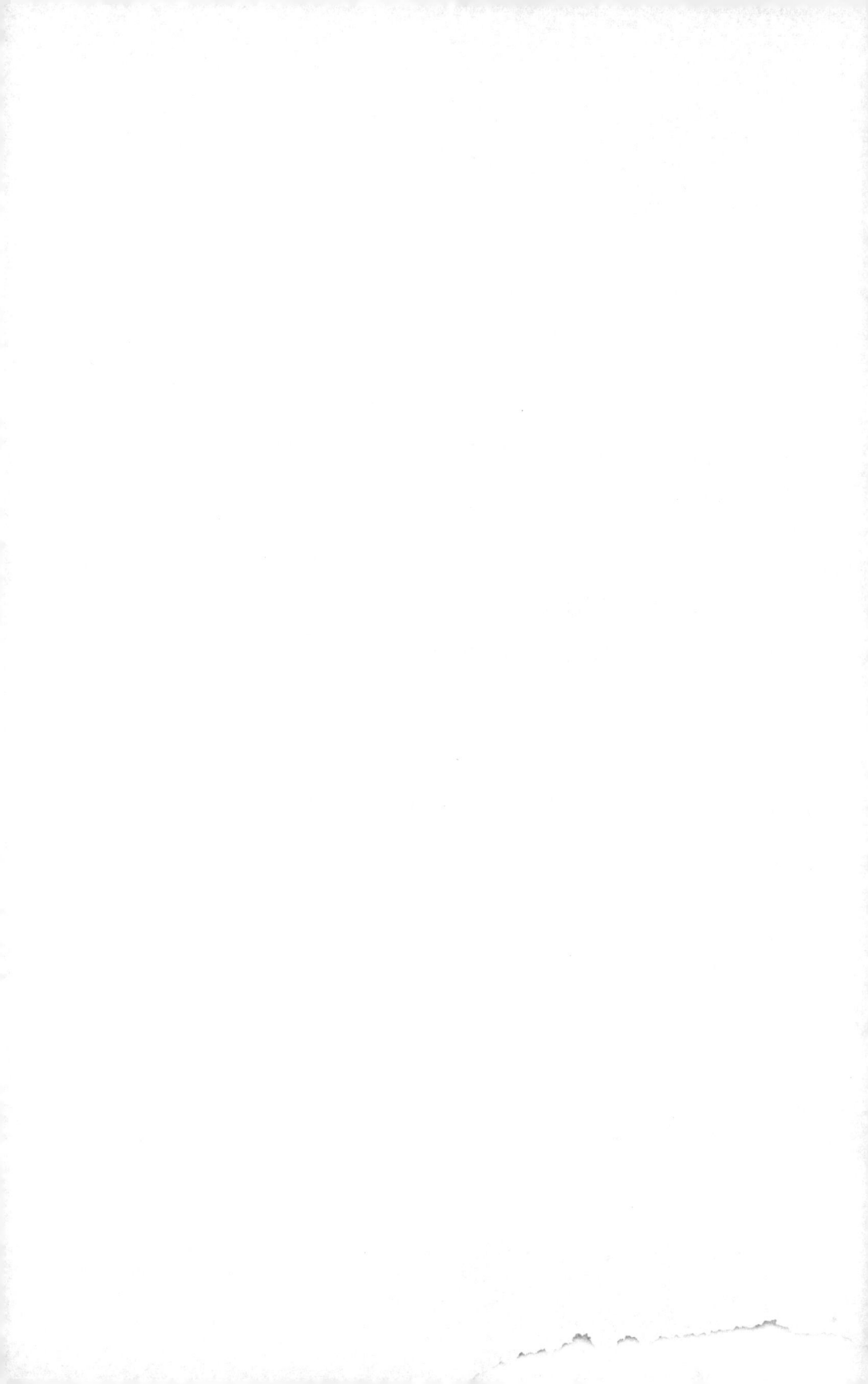

the world is heavy.

and we carry its weight

not with our hands

but our hearts.

a heavy weightless thing

it comes slowly and silently. with autumn cloud tenderness. warm handed it will hold you caress and lull you softly into its sleep. or it comes all together at once. loud and sudden. like thunder. violent like a fist that hits whilst you are looking the other way. whilst you are dreaming. of tomorrow. it will grab the future from your vision until you can see only today.

it is heavy. like the heaviest weightless thing you have ever carried. the burden of it will not fall upon your hands and shake it nor upon your back and break it. it will be heavy *within* you. like smog. like a dead thing; alive but dying. like how the first breath and the last breath is the same; and in the moment of it, it is difficult to tell which is which.

it will rest upon your bones and tell you that *you are not moving today.* the message comes from a full empty place. a faceless face; nothing seen. and a voiceless voice; nothing heard but it is clear and it is there. *you are not moving today.* and you will not move. your veins will become hollow like abandoned temples once filled with prayer. not even prayer will move you. and what is prayer if there is no god? and what is atheism if there is one? that thing you were looking forward to suddenly becomes burden so you will make excuses. *i am not feeling well; i am not feeling myself. i am not feeling.* but then you remember their face and see how it looks at you when you are not there when you said you would be. their face now reminds you of how you feel inside and because you know how it feels to feel this way and you do not want them to feel this way so you go, to that *thing*. and they, they only feel this way on their face but you, you feel this way in your bones. and it grinds you. all the way to dust. so you go. to that *thing*. and there you are. moveless. though you thought you beat it, didn't you? at least for today you thought you beat that voice without a voice when you went but it was right when it said *you are not moving today* because you went to this *thing* and you did not move, just like it said. you were there and you did not move. there are times when you will move but even in your moving you are moveless, for the times when you move and you think you have beaten it by moving you eventually realise that your moving was on the outside. that even in the moment of your moving, your inside does not move and you feel this. you feel this when your moving is finished and you go back to being still. to it being right. that voice without a voice. it speaks. but for a moment you were happy because they were happy. for they saw you move

but did not know that your moving was not like theirs though it looked the part.

and you give yourself to your destruction because the fall is much easier than the climb. the fall is weightless. a perpetual freedom. the ground is closer to touch than the sky, so why reach up? why when you will never be able to feel the sky? the sky envelopes. the sky consumes. it is heavy. and this, this is the root of your affliction; knowing that you are nothing but this destruction but at the same time infinitely more than it ; knowing that you cannot escape it - your destruction - for if you do it will push you further away from them. further on your own. your freedom is liberating. a weightlessness all of its own but it comes not without pain for the pain is knowing that you are alone in this. and though your lonesomeness soothes you it is also your breaking for no one was born to be alone. too well, you know this. we are born, we die, and during, we rest in between the tender balance of things. of all things. though we wish to be we are never quite alone. and though we wish to be we are never quite included. we exist on the peripheries; this tender balance. we carry the degrees of its experience and it rests heavy in us. on us. of us. it takes too much and gives too little yet we feel it all. a heavy weightless thing. if only you knew that it too breathes. like you. that it's infinite expanding is like your lungs and the air it breathes is the ethereal star dust of the universe. it feels and suffers like you. like you it is the bearer of pain and not just its own. it harbours the pain of those who do not have their stories told; the silenced; the muted; the forgotten. and that's why it is heavy on you because you feel their pain; those whose suffering makes a song in the ears of the deaf and their dancing rythymless feet tramples all over its melody. their pain makes you feel more of your own and so you feel more

of theirs. and more of your own. and more of theirs. it is chemical melancholy. and that's

why it is beautiful for it does not look at itself with a greater beauty than it looks at others. it's shining is not from its own light. if only you knew that you that it is neither your light nor your darkness that scares. it is the beauty of the gentle balance between; this hard softness; this tender strength. that you may find it there. and it, like you, rests in the gentle balance of all things. so do not just give yourself to one way or too much, to one thing. do not let despair be the heavy upon your soul without hope being the wings that lifts it up. do not stay still.

what is?

there were times when i tried

to squeeze out my last breath

with the palm of my hands. times

when each sunset reminded me of death.

like the world was slowly closing its eyes

into an eternal sleep. sunrise

was a promise that i did not want to keep.

i walked with my deepest fears in each step.

too afraid to walk right. i walked

until there was nothing left.

this path is not one that i chose.

it is one that i came to find. it is not one that i own.

it belongs to the generation of souls laid to rest

at the bottom of the ocean. and rose again

until they became the clouds in our skies. raining down

on us with forgiveness for all our sins of

forgetting their struggle

and leaving it all behind.

i walk blind. because sometimes

tomorrow is too far to see. so i walk

with one hand out hoping that if i could

touch it before i see it

maybe it will be that much more real to me.

but what is real to me?

when the same friend i heard singing my praises

turned out to be my enemy.

what is family? when i see my brothers

stab one another. look him in the eyes

and steal the last words on his lips?

what if those last words were poetry?

what is royalty? if when i told her she was a Queen she

said she'd rather be a bad bitch.

and when i told him that he was King

he said he'd rather be a pimp.

we turn our hearts into stone.

so every time it beats it is an earthquake

turning to ruins the abandoned cities inside us

where we walk alone.

what is fear? if when i walked down

the narrow street i saw 12 boys with their hoods up

and i called them gods because that's what they were.

and deep in their eyes i could see a reflection of me;

scared.

i told them *i'm sorry this world hates you*

and it will bring you down to your knees

but you are giants so always remember

to stand tall on your feet.

and in the darkness of that night

they took a little bit of their light.

broke it and said *do this in remembrance of me.*

what is pain? what is hurt?

what is hope? what is love?

do not think of giving up.

know that inside of us there are a billion

stars. and we are walking constellations.

a moving homage to the glory of the universe.

the most beautiful things in this world have questions that
we will never know the answer to but that doesn't take
away from its beauty.

you are beautiful, child.

there is life in you.

and you are still the most complicated question

that i am trying to find the answer to.

missing peace

who's to blame
when a young girl looks in the mirror
and only sees her imperfections?
that she is not the right shape size or shade
or thin enough to fit into the narrow space
created by society's shrinking minds.
that when she grows up she would have changed
so much of herself that she will become a stranger
to her own childhood eyes. recognise.
who's to blame when boys are taught to validate
their existence through violence or meaningless sex?
neglect their emotions until they become men.
90% perpetrators of all violent crime.

but what do we expect when people feed on lies
and are starved of the truth?
where's the proof that we are alive?

that there is a beating heart underneath

this burnt flesh. this burnt flesh that gave birth

to the rest. who's to blame

when this knowledge is missing in school

text books or when a child doesn't want to read?

look. <u>education</u> begins when you leave school.

so read. read. read until it hurts you

and your eyes begin to bleed

because you feel the pain of the words.

the pain of this poetry.

who's to blame when a boy walks hood up

jeans sag low, middle finger to the world?

just because nobody listens. because nobody cares.

who's to blame when that boy is your cousin?

your nephew? your son? who's to blame that boy was you?

only 10 years ago. that you walk on road

and play Russian roulette with your life

but the only reason you screw up your face and stare is

because you want someone to notice you are alive.

who do you turn to when life gets too much?

when you feel your clutch begin to weaken

as you struggle to hold on?

who's to blame when you fall

and no one is there to catch you?

when your fears attack you

and depression begins to relax you

into an early grave?

we kill ourselves as much as we kill each other

but nobody wants to talk about suicide

because its seen as a weakness. so we bury

these feelings deep inside and try to mask ourselves

but the strongest person is the one

who can admit when they need help.

so when i call you brother or sister

it's not because i'm down

or to try to appear cool

it's because i look at where you are

and i see i've been there too.

i've swallowed anger

and spat out rage. felt the fire burn

in the pit of my stomach

until i threw up the flames.

i used to clench my fists to fight

but now i clench my fists to write.

so tell me why my fists keep writing?

maybe it's the rage that lives inside me.

maybe it's the peace that's trying to find me.

maybe if we all gave a little piece of ourselves

to each other, we'd be whole again.

looking for god

in life

when you have stared adversity in the face

with its beady eyes and snarling teeth

and smiled. when you have decided

that you can no longer walk the path of others

instead you set your own. your feet

set trails of blazing glory and fire into the ground.

when you can no longer tolerate injustice.

and would rather die on your feet

than live on your knees.

and you would sacrifice it all

to know what it means to be free.

remember those moments when you have felt peace.

it's melody has played in your ear

and brought dreams to your sleep.

because in life all you need is a dream.

and for when a dream is all you have.

but you still hold on.

when nobody believes in you.

but you still hold on.

when temptation makes you weak.

but you still stay strong.

when you have sat near angels or amongst strangers and you have seen no difference in either. when you have stopped on your way to work to talk to that homeless guy you ignore too often just to ask how is their day. and you don't even care whether or not you'll be late.

when you look a child in their eyes

and see a reflection of yourself.

you see that the innocence of youth

does not make them naive but instead it's a virtue.

when you see old age not as a burden

but something to aspire to.

when you can look back on the future

and ahead to the past. and you understand

that the present is the only time that lasts.

when you have seen with your mind and felt with your heart.

when you understand that all people are equal.

and when that person walks down the road and you see them no stereotypes come to mind.

when you understand that the world wasn't made in six days for it still isn't finished.

that we haven't reached the end times

this is only the beginning.

when you see the sunrise before the dawn.

beauty in all its forms.

when you know that life does not imitate art.

and art does not imitate life.

life *is* art. art *is* life.

and we create with each moment that passes by.

when you understand that love

is not something that you fall in

it is something that you become.

it is what you are. it is what you do.

that's when you would have found god.

that's when you would have found you.

man, listen

women belong in two places,

either the bedroom or the kitchen

he said laughing and then looked at me like

i should agree with him.

at that moment i felt sorry for the mother

who raised him and the daughter he may one day have.

i wanted to apologise to every woman in the room because

as the only two guys there our shared gender did not mean

our shared thinking. so i told him

'man, listen,

you've been conditioned

with hyper masculine patriarchal contradictions like you

probably want a woman who is a freak in the sheets

but still a virgin. you want to pay for everything to assert

your masculinity but when a woman doesn't pay you claim

she's a gold digger.

you say women should dress modestly

and not reveal their bodies

but secretly you still endorse pornography.

silently you tell women to act like a lady

but think like a man are you looking for a wife or one of

your bredrins?

man, listen

this isn't your fantasy, this is dangerous thinking. you've

painted a picture of every woman being the same because

there's only one kind you can deal with. ran away from the

ones

you could have kept it real with.

so disillusioned by the lies.

do you even know

what the real is?

man, listen

i heard your jokes about feminism

but men need feminism too

because men commit suicide

at three times the higher rate than women do.

so if showing emotions is such a sign of weakness

why does it literally kill us to cry?

why do you say that you are scared

to have a daughter

because you know what men are like?

why not instead raise sons that act right?

man, listen

so nobody sat down with you

and told you about what being a man means.

and you were raised on commercial hip hop misogyny

phony television series and

hollywood movies without anyone to tell you the reality.

well consider that person me.

a man is one when he knows how to be tender

in times of tenderness and strong in times of strength.

it is not about how much you can lift

but how much you can give

when there's nothing left.

when your glass heart

has been broken into a thousand pieces

how strong will you be to pick up each piece

and love again?

man, listen

this poem isn't for us. it's for our future sons who deserve

not to be raised like us.

the ones who will grow up with hearts that

are numb drowning in shallow lies

because they listen to people like you

who told them how they should feel inside.

and i know it's much more complicated than this. more

than what this poem could accomplish but sometimes i

wish

we would just listen.

you are a silent revolution.

a star being born into the sky.

if you want to be loved

be soft. softer. softer, still.
make yourself tenderness
until you can be held.

they only miss you when you're gone

but i miss you
whilst you are still
here. in my presence.
smell your hair
and touch your skin.
hear your voice. kiss your lips
knowing that one day
i will not be able to.

alone

when i am alone
i want the silence of this house
to be filled
with your quiet.

to those with wings for feet who keep on running

most days

i spend my days trying to figure out

what the days mean and i'm stuck.

stuck between caring too much and not caring enough.

between holding on too long and letting go too easily feet

stumbling beneath me trying to follow this narrow path.

i look around

and all i see are faces that laugh

grass greener on the other side. eyes wide

brimming smiles. full hearts. music on blast

and the nervous excitement from the accidental

touch of two lovers at the start.

i look at myself and i'm going nowhere. fast.

maybe this is just a façade.

a shallow mask to cover up the fact that

we are all hurting inside.

that no amount of pride could dry

the sea of tears. years of pain.

waiting for clouds to clear. fear

settling like dust. and you know what?

some days i am just tired.

some days i'm barely strong enough

to carry the burden of this heavy heart

let alone the weight of the world on my shoulders.

some days i need some space on my own.

no internet. no mobile phone.

some days i just want to run away from it all.

but then on some days i hear a voice call

in the back of my mind each syllable sounds like a little

droplet of light falling

on deaf eyes that wander through the darkness and it says

to me

why would you want to run when you have wings for feet?
fly.

so this is to all those with wings for feet who keep on
running please do not run, fly.

fly like the poets pen off the page.

fly like it was your 12th birthday and you just made the
biggest wish and blew out a candle with a flame the size of
the sun. and the darkness of the universe
is now your living room.

fly like a midnight moonlight city cyclist
with headphones on going downhill
with no hands.

fly

like a runner

in the park racing against the sunset.

no regrets like every mistake you ever made

has just been washed away.

fly like your new crush has just noticed you looking fly

and has walked up to you holding

roses and chocolates to ask you out on a date

and they're paying.

fly like you never stopped believing in love

like you weren't the only one.

there was a time when everything you imagined was real.

your mind is the most powerful instrument you will ever

own. only second to your heart which you feel and they are

made of one and the same, so fly.

fly like you are not worried about the days

months and years of getting older

because each day you live is the youngest you will ever be.

we live eternally. in each dream. in each sleep we keep a

piece of ourselves to give to each other.

so this is to all those with wings for feet who keep on

running

please do not run, fly.

save you

you might need this poem

to lift you up. to remove the heavy

brought on from the sorrows of the world.

to relieve you. to peace together each broken

piece of your soul.

making you whole from everything that keeps

tearing you apart. when you lie sleepless at night

trying to find the reasons to keep up the fight

you might need this poem to remind you

that in the end, everything will be alright.

so if it's not alright, it's not the end.

i contemplated suicide. until one day i realised

that many already die before they are dead and being

alive does not mean you are living. death begins with

the mind. and too often we already kill ourselves

just from what we think. then the body simply follows

how we feel inside.

you might need this poem to give you hope

when your back is against the ropes.

everything you swallow tastes like lead.

when you choke on air and the voices echo

in your head. when each step feels so heavy.

when each breath feels so heavy.

and you don't know if it's the last one you have left. you

might need this poem to remind you that each breath is the

only one you have left because we can only live in the

moment.

our lives are golden but too often

we live in the darkness of our fears

worrying so much about a future that

may never come. my friend died. he was only 32 years. i

remember. on the platform of a train station. when we last

spoke he had a light in his eyes as he told me of a new
beginning.
who knew so soon that he was going to a different place
where we will all one day go but until then

you might need this poem to save you.

what if when we die we become another star in the universe and heaven is just the beautiful constellation of all our souls?

something beautiful

something beautiful is happening
right here. right now. in this room.
lifting the gloom from our consciousness
like when the light of the moon
reflects off open water into the night.
something beautiful is happening.
caterpillar to butterfly. rose blossom.
spring bloom. two star crossed lovers' eyes
meet for the first time from across the room.
i dreamed when i was two my grandmother
sat me on her knee and said
mokili oyo ezali ya yo
na maloba na yo oko komisa yango kitoko.

and just like you i didn't understand what was she said
but the feeling stayed with me
and when i got older i asked my father and he replied

your grandmother talked because she didn't have much time left.

 i haven't seen her since
but wherever she is, she stays with me
a woman that i never knew.

on that day
something beautiful happened
when i first wrote poetry. the ground
no longer knew the weight of my feet.
i felt my soul rise
eternally. my footprints
were erased from the earth's memory.
i started at infinity and retraced my steps
back to the beginning
so i knew both where i was going
and where i had come from.

where i belong

to the constellation of dying stars

whose light does not shine bright enough

for this world to see.

because like the universe i am mostly darkness

and darkness dwells alone

in the corners of dimly lit rooms

or the backs of your mind.

darkness is unknown. undiscovered. unrelenting.

something beautiful is happening

the way our imagination catches fire

when we dream. so let these words be the match

our breath is the spark

that we may set our future to light

bring it to life from the dark. let us dance.

the way that children do.

the way the deaf move to a baseline

they feel only in their soul.

the way my heart beats for you, world.

dream.

it is a declaration to your spirit

that you are alive

and you will never give up.

treat every obstacle like a door

and just walk through it.

place your hands underneath your head

when you sleep at night

so that you may hold on to your dreams.

and never. *never.* let them go.

though i, like you, am filled with fear

and my heart trembles like my hands

but thought they are shaking i dare not let go.

never let go.

know that your being here right now

is by no accident. we will all find our way

back home. but when you arrive leave your fears

at the door and wipe away all of your tears

because we have cried for too long

after all of these years. so when you return know

that only love is welcome here.

love.

love is something beautiful.

it is the echoes of our beating hearts in silent solitude and

in the stillness. where one day

we will find ourselves.

remember me

who will remember us?

the quiet of voice. the soft of heart.

us who would rather part from the path of pain

but would risk it all just to feel again.

who will remember us?

we walk down corridors ignored

as if we are one with the walls.

we are the dreamers

wishing our lives away. the pain

of seeing this world not as it is

but as it should be lives with us.

in our minds we create

a sanctuary. a solitude. where our souls

are grown kept awake late at night

by our thoughts just so we can go. to *there*.

to find peace

whilst the world sleeps. we

who wear our hearts not on our sleeves

but in our poetry.

in each breath

these words that linger on the edge

of our tongues; words that are never said.

so we write

because nobody is listening.

nobody hears our silence.

i write because i have nobody to talk to.

walk through each step heavy

like our conscience

the monsters that lurk in the back

of our minds

like fear. rage. love. this is our story.

rip every page out

and spread them across the bed

like rose petals.

stand in your beauty

and show it to your lover.

the only miracle is how we survive this world.

more war

more bombs. air strikes. drones.

more guns. bullets tear bodies.

breaks bones. blood flows

through streets. out homes. more

refugees. families forced to flee.

remember little boy face down

by the sea? and your heavy heart.

what would he say to you now

if he could speak? more

dead women and children. because

they have not suffered enough.

'minimise casualties' is okay

as long as it's not one of us. more

ashes to ashes and dreams to dust.

nightmares during sunrise,

it feeds their rush.

their fire. their flame. their heat.

more war, more war, more war,

for more peace.

we are dying (we live)

every moment we are dying.
we are but fading star being
wished upon to make the dreams
of a lost lover come true or a
child who wished nothing more
than to see peace at home,
instead of war, instead of fists
on faces turned blue from sorrow.
i only live for today because some
days, i wish not see tomorrow, so
i tell people i love them daily
for if today is the last day i see
at least i know they will have a
a peace of me.
every moment we are dying.
and we do not know when.
how many breaths can we count until

the end. this tender balance;
a trembling hand holding us close
between life and death, there is a
prayer held between touching palms
that kiss like lovers lips,
on bended knees, wishing for a future
with us inside of it, that we are there
living, breathing, free.
but every moment we are dying
and we do not know when
so take this moment, here and now
breathe life into it, build it a temple
go inside and pray, to a god that has
the faces of everyone you love,
touch every string with your fingertips
and play your song, take these brushes
and paint the world beautiful,

bring colour to the dullness

for every moment we are dying,

but for this, right here, right now,

we live.

love by design

will never forget

that night

looking out past

moon light

to sacred heart

and sacred body

praising the architecture of both.

she is a poem

she is not a poet. she is a poem

writing herself into the hearts

of everything she touches

but she wouldn't have you know it.

her story is untold

like a flower that never unfolds

to the sun, she has no option but

to search for the light within herself.

her spirit is her wealth

the most precious natural resource,

she holds a nation in her palm.

calmed the cries of orphaned babies

and wiped away their tears.

in spite of the suffering and the violence

after all these years

she has vowed never to let go,

so with hope she keeps holding on.

you cannot speak to me of being strong

until you have heard the laughter

of a rape survivor caress your spine.

it will paralyse your indifference.

the sunset of her smile

will stay forever in your mind

until that day when you realise

that you are much closer connected

than you think. because when on the brink

of despair everybody stares into the horizon

dreaming of a better day.

if only she could write her own future.

but she isn't a poet, she is a poem

being written into your heart.

signs

when the fisherman returns

after the water has dried and the dead

carcass of our hopes lay floating in the shallow.

the sun barely touches our skin and leaves us

in the shadow of our fears, the flowers wilting

in the darkness bowing, bowing, to a floating moon.

a god that does not know the names it has thrown

into the wind, carrying your prayers to a place

you will never see. and the silent prayer, a quiet plea

that never leaves your heart; cold metal on the temple

click in the ear. no funeral.

dreams melt into a pool of nightmares

from which we drink to quench our thirst,

our parched lips speak of things not even we believe

the future, slips away from our fingertips, we have nothing

to hold on to but the hands of the people who abandon us

when we need them most. the morning comes,
the dust settles but still you cannot see.
their eyes. hollow mouths. faces disguised. hearts
that do not beat. feet marching back, marching back
into defeat. freedom is a long walk. one day you will see.
those who do not see will feel. those who do not feel will
not heal. and those who do not heal are marching back,
marching back into.

the sign will come that day when the sky burns. you will
hear the whisper in your ear, it is time to go. on that day
you must leave.

i have heard it.

Translations

- **l'humanité** (pg. 61)

The above poem is written in French. A translation of the title is 'humanity', in English. A brief summary of the poem is that it is a reflection on the current state of humanity; this is portrayed in the first line of the opening stanza, 'l'humanité est perdue', which translates to 'humanity is lost', and the next stanza begins 'une nature corrompue', which translates to 'a corrupted nature' and the next line that follows is 'led by hate and greed. Though quite a pessimist or realist start to the poem, which continues, there is a positive twist where the contributions of humanity is considered ; 'on a construit des pyramides/ c'était les étoiles qui nous guidaient/ une puissance solaire. divine.' This roughly translates to, 'we built the pyramids, we were guided by the stars, a solar power divine.' The poem then raises questions urging that a choice must be made ;

'des cauchemars ou des rêves ? l'amour ou la haine ?', which translates to 'nightmares or dreams ? love or hate ?' The poem then concludes as a plea that humanity must return.

- **something beautiful** (pg. 109)

mokili oyo ezali ya yo
na maloba na yo oko komisa yango kitoko.

This excerpt from the above poem is written in Lingala, native to D.R. Congo. The rough translation is, 'the world is yours, with your words you will make it beautiful.'

JJ Bola
Writer | Poet |Educator| Human
Also the writer of poetry collections *Elevate, Daughter of the Sun* (e-book) and forthcoming novel *No Place to Call Home*.

In March 2016 WORD was accepted into the Poetry Library collection at the Royal Festival Hall. If you enjoyed reading this book, let people know! Share your thoughts on social media, recommend to friends or family, and review online. Visit **www.jjbola.com** for more information, videos, pictures, or to get in touch. Thank you.